ARCHITECTURE IN PERSPECTIVE 8

A Competitive Exhibition Of Architectural Delineation

Chicago Architecture Foundation, Chicago, Illinois
October—November, 1993

Center For Creative Studies, College of Art and Design, Detroit, Michigan
April, 1994—June, 1994

A.I.A. National Convention, Los Angeles, California
May 13—16, 1994

For the past seven years, *Architecture In Perspective* exhibitions have been successfully displayed by notable Museums, Institutions, Universities, Galleries and A.I.A. Chapter offices throughout the United States and Canada, ASAP would welcome any inquiries of interest from any organization about hosting future shows.

The American Society of Architectural Perspectivists

Pomegranate Artbooks / San Francisco

Best of Show Awards

Lee Dunnette, AIA—*Worth Square Building, 1986*

James Record—*The State Capitol, 1986*

Hugh Ferriss Memorial Prize Winners

Richard Lovelace—*One Montvale Avenue, 1987*

Thomas W. Schaller, AIA—*Cultural Center, 1988*

Daniel E. Willis—*Edgar Allan Poe Memorial, 1989*

Gilbert Gorski, AIA—*The Basilica Ulpia, 1990*

Luis Blanc—*Affordable Housing Now!, 1991*

Douglas Jamieson—*BMC Real Properties Building, 1992*

The Hugh Ferriss Memorial Prize, awarded annually for excellence in the graphic representation of architecture, is sustained by the continued sponsorship of the Van Nostrand Reinhold Company, New York City.

This exhibition catalog of Architecture In Perspective was produced with the assistance and professional skills of the following individuals—*Art Director:* Dario Tainer, AIA, Chicago; *Layout and Production Coordination:* John Deputy, MetroDesign, Boston; *Copywriting and Editing:* Frank Costantino, Boston; Gordon Grice, OAA, MRAIC, Toronto; Thomas Schaller, AIA, New York; Dario Tainer, AIA, Chicago; *Jury Evaluations:* Ms. Bonnie Wolf, AIA, Walter Netsch, FAIA, Jack O. Hedrich, all of Chicago; *Commentaries:* AIP 8 Selected Artists; *Compilation and Transcription Coordination:* Eliza Beckwith, New York; Catherine Costantino, Boston; Roberta Danko, Chicago; Nancy Kilmartin, Boston. The funding for this catalog and exhibition is provided, in part, by each of the selected member artists.

Published by Pomegranate Artbooks, Box 6099, Rohnert Park, CA 94927

Exhibition Framing by Frame Central, Boston, MA

Official ASAP Shipping Agent: U.S. Art, Boston, MA

Cover: David Sylvester, *Tuckerton Marine Research Field Station*

ISBN 1-56640-678-1

F o r e w o r d

This year's International Competition mirrored the state of the Illustrator's art and the state of their world. And yet again, it proved that the Society's acronym, ASAP, is a very appropriate one indeed.

Obliged to reschedule the competition earlier in the year because of catalog printing and publishing time frames, the Society invited submissions of their members best work ASAP! Already accustomed to such schedules for their own clients, some 121 members—a fair number from such distant places as Australia, Japan, Saudi Arabia, France, Malta, in addition to continental members in Canada and the U.S.—sent 367 slides to be closely scrutinized, critiqued, analyzed, and hopefully selected by the AIP 8 jury.

True to form, the jurors expended much effort discussing viewpoint, technique, light and shadow, contextualism, and, as later proved the case, appropriateness. Their most difficult task was applying an assumed special criteria of "balance between elegance and exuberance" for selecting a show that best described today's field. As discussions ensued, the dynamic tension and resolution of such concepts became evident in the personal pursuits of the jurors themselves.

The developing focus that became clearer during the course of their deliberations was the jury's architectural preferences for science and research facilities, sports and leisure proposals, and a predominance of residential projects. As a result, there was a marked absence of commercial designs, especially high-rises. Within the total scope of entries, the submissions truly captured the current worldwide crisis in the real estate industry. Despite the scarcity of "noteworthy" (i.e. large-scale urban) architecture, the jurors were not disappointed in the material, as the quality of the work reached new heights.

Continually reminding one another of their charge to assemble a rich and varied show, the jury agonized over each and every slide, to the point that some early dismissed works were recovered for reconsideration, and either selected for another round or re-rejected.

The end result of this refined process represents a moment in time, a snapshot album of superb drawings from professionals around the world, who labor under tight deadlines and sometimes shrinking budgets, but never relinquish their love of drawing and their aspirations to strive for excellence and mastery of technique.

You will find AIP 8 a most introspective exhibition as the boundaries between architectural illustration and art become ever so closely intertwined.

Dario Tainer, AIA
President, American Society of
Architectural Perspectivists
Chicago, June 1993

Introduction

Walter A. Netsch, FAIA

Bonnie J. Wolf, AIA

Jack O. Hedrich

Continuing a tradition established over the past seven years, a very unusual group of professionals convened in the sumptuous, elegant and comfortable surroundings of the media center at the Chicago headquarters of Miglin Beitler Incorporated. A prestigious and influential development company, Miglin-Beitler has helped transform the Chicago sky-line into one of the most balanced and aesthetically pleasing sky-lines in the world. Prior to the judging of this year's submission, the jury and ASAP coordinators were treated to the presentation drawings and models for the company's current project for the tallest building in the world—a rather appropriate introduction to the power that architectural illustrations possess in portraying the shape of todays' (or tomorrow's) built environment.

Selected for their diverse, yet appropriate interests in architecture generally, and architectural illustration in particular, this eighth *Architecture In Perspective* jury had direct applicable experience in the technical aspects of perspective drawing, its artistic execution, and its subliminal use as a powerful marketing tool.

Walter A. Netsch, FAIA, former partner with Skidmore Owing and Merrill, former Chicago Park District Commissioner, distinguished planner, award winning architect, renown lecturer and teacher, art collector, and accomplished painter in his own right, joined Ms. Bonnie J. Wolf, AIA, formerly of SOM, and currently one of Miglin's Beitler's architectural coordinators for their commercial development. With a trained architectural eye tempered by a developmental viewpoint, Ms. Wolf was well familiar with the necessity of strong architectural presentations. She was also chosen as chair for the jury.

The third and final member of the jury, Mr. Jack O. Hedrich, founder of one of the country's most prestigious architectural photography studios, comfortably adopted his day's role. Over nearly three decades, he also was confronted with the challenging aspects of viewpoint, selection of media, and angle of lighting inherent in capturing an architectural form, its essence and its setting. Despite the differences in medium and time frame (built vs. unbuilt, existing vs planned) for the photographer, it is exactly those qualities that confront the architectural illustrator with each new commission.

After viewing the first round of some 367 submissions, the jury immediately remarked (not unlike their predecessors) on the difficulty of selecting sixty works from such a wide range of subject matter, technique, and styles. They did concur that their role, as Chair Wolf observed, "was to assemble a rich and varied exhibition that would adequately illustrate a cross section of the material...and at the same time maintain or elevate the quality level commonly associated with ASAP."

As one powerful image after another flickered on the screen, a recurring question was discussed by the jury— is it architectural drawing or is it art? In many cases, much time was spent looking beyond the marvelously illustrated perspectives and delving into the message that seemed to be subtlely conveyed by the artists and their interpretation of the projects. The winning entries epitomized and punctuated their discussions as each image carried beyond simply representing a building masterfully. Social consciousness and hope for the future, for example, exude from the Hugh Ferriss Memorial Prize winner's drawing, while a romantic ideal was coupled with a creative and multi-functional solution in the Formal Category selection. The Informal Category winner "recycled" material and presented a collage of ideas and styles, reflecting the purpose behind the building design, while the individual Juror Awards were chosen for their artistic, stylistic correctness, powerful visual handling and necessary contextualism.

Constantly searching for what Juror Netsch termed "a balance between elegance and exuberance," the gradually coalesced jury concluded their intense ten hour deliberation with a new and deep appreciation for the efforts of the architectural illustrator. In a veritable melange of visual proficiency, the exhibition demonstrated on one level both the differences as well as the similarities of architectural solutions from around the world. On a more technical level, the selected professionals had unfailingly mastered their methods. As for the drawings' value as art, appropriately enough, the eye of each beholder will undoubtedly ascertain that quality as this remarkable display travels the world.

The distinguished jurors of *Architecture In Perspective 8* were unanimous in their selection of a work by New Jersey artist David Sylvester to be honored with the American Society of Architectural Perspectivists' most prestigious award, entitled "Tuckerton Marine Research Station". The piece was praised by Juror Wolf for its "display of sheer dexterity, in all senses of the word; adroit and clever in the use of both hand and mind…its other-wordliness which lies directly beneath the surface of a scene we all think we recognize." The jurors were impressed with the highly-textured color pencil drawing, charged as it is with depth, subtle meaning and mystery, and to the juror's observations, not unlike an Andrew Wyeth painting. It was however, the concept of dialogue which (by thc artist's admission) most informed the work—the dialogue between artist and client, artist and his work and ultimately between architecture and its site. As illustrated by the following artist/client exchange, Mr. Sylvester was so moved by the beauty of the site and the sensitivity of the proposed design that he felt the ultimate work of art all but "completed itself", making verbal dialogue almost superfluous:

Architect: "David, these are existing conditions drawings. Rutgers bought this property for use as a research facility, but the conditions are sub-standard with insufficient space for their needs. The structures represent an historical vernacular building type, and are an important part of the local traditions and landscape. Our charge is to preserve the character of the existing architecture while getting as much research ability as the site will allow."

Sylvester: "I see."

Architect: "Here are some photos. The site is on coastal marshland between Great Bay and the Atlantic. All the structures are built on a wood pile platform, so building area is very limited. The only access is by a 1/4 mile long boardwalk. We will be restoring the main building to its original state. The boathouse will get a second story and a new roof. The laboratory building will also get a second floor and new roof with added dormers to match the main building…"

Sylvester: "A salt marsh?"

Architect: "Yes, that's right…the character of the landscape is important to this project. The marsh is expansive with no nearby trees or buildings to lend scale to these structures. The weather, colors, lighting and tides are constantly changing. So, bearing all this in mind, we need to show as many of our proposed changes as possible in one view. How would you approach a rendering of this project?…David?"

Sylvester: "Incredible…"

With a clarity of hindsight to better inform his response, Mr. Sylvester reflected, "I was increasingly captivated by the special circumstances of this project as the architect was describing them. Clear direction and strong inspiration do not often come so quickly upon introduction to a rendering problem. In this case, the image formed in my mind's eye as the client spoke and was essentially complete before he inquired about my approach. There was another conversation expressed in this drawing— the non-verbal dialogue between human activity and what we perceive as the natural world. The Tuckerton research facility is dedicated to the study and understanding of the environment upon which it stands with such clear and dramatic contrast. The viewer might wonder—to what extent is this field station part of the natural environment, and as such, is it beautiful?"

The effectiveness and clarity of Mr. Sylvester's dialogue with both the client and his own craft created a subtle form of drawing beauty well deserving of the jurors' selection as recipient of ASAP's highest honor.

441 Vannest Avenue
Trenton, New Jersey 08618
609.882.4360

D a v i d   S y l v e s t e r

Additions and Renovations to Tuckerton Marine Research Field Station
Architects: Saphire Associates P.C.

Color pencil on illustration board, 16x20, 1992

"A painting that masters perspective in composition and content" wrote Juror Bonnie Wolf of Thomas Schaller's watercolor, "Proposed Residential Span"—winner of the AIP 8 Formal Category Award. Aside from technical merit, the jurors especially admired the sense of narrative and the range of ideas from formal concept to subtle humor which pervades and informs the work.

The bridge as a subject for artistic and architectural investigation has long fascinated Mr. Schaller who is taken with the beauty of its conceptual simplicity. "It has," he stated, "in most cases a single function—to vault space in order to facilitate movement from one point to another. Yet nothing in the built environment speaks the language of movement so eloquently". However, it was the idea of the bridge as both "transitional element" and "place of arrival" that most inspired this piece. Schaller was intrigued by the fact that while historic spans such as the Ponte Vecchio in Venice, London's Tower Bridge and the Charles Bridge in Prague have long been used as centers for social or commercial gatherings, few modern examples exist of the bridge as "emblematic of both *journey and destination*."

Of his winning work Mr. Schaller stated: "The structure attempts to respect its site by minimizing land coverage and, in its usage of form, by a symbolic nod to the flat-topped buttes and natural land bridges of the region. The vertical piers spring in form and intent from the warm-hued stones of the landscape, while the horizontal components of the roadway span and actual residential units are comprised of the cooler tones of more light-weight materials—steel, aluminum and glass. Finally, the great arch formed by the geometry of unit placement indirectly expresses the structure within while affording a celebration of the vast negative space created."

Beyond the skillful use of the watercolor medium, it was the multi-layered story told by this work which most attracted the jurors—a fantasy of both architecture and human experience. "The landscape and colors," noted Juror Wolf, "the appearance of the figures in the foreground make us discoverers in a great adventure... one immediately shares in the hikers' amazement."

2112 Broadway #407
New York, New York 10023
212.362.5524

Thomas Schaller, AIA

Proposed Residential Span
Architect: Thomas Wells Schaller, AIA

Watercolor, 25x18, 1993

Since the introduction of the category divisions in 1989, some confusion has yet to be dispelled over what distinguishes "formal" from "informal" rendering. Clarity on the distinction varies from year to year, depending on the jury, and even judges within a given jury may not agree on a given work. This year's selection may do little to clear up the confusion. Clearly, the category distinction is intended to encourage submissions of the widest variety of architectural representation, irrespective of category, and not differentiate between commissioned work and theoretical work.

This year's Informal Category winner, Texas architect/educator/illustrator Richard Ferrier, has been for some years involved in what he describes as "an ongoing investigation of architectural potential." Referring to his highly organized abstract drawings and constructions: "(They) provide us with a method of exploring the juxtaposition of architectural considerations;" and with respect to *Windows and Fragments,* "...architectural components, the landscape and windows, which allow a vision into and out of reality, to provoke intellectual as well as intuitive response".

Where the preponderance of architectural representation is highly referential and strictly representational, Mr. Ferrier's intentionally ambiguous work was greatly admired by the Chicago jury. In appreciation of its exceptional artistic merit, they were unanimous in awarding it the distinction of Best Informal Category Submission.

School of Architecture, Box 19108
University of Texas
Arlington, Texas 76019
817.273.2315

R i c h a r d   B .   F e r r i e r ,   F A I A

Windows and Fragments: The Picturesque
Architects: Ferrier, Hampton, Quevedo, King

Graphite, watercolor, metals and photographic film, 30x40, 1991

Inspiration for architectural illustration may derive from many sources. After more than half a century, the visionary work of Russian Constructivist architect, Ivan Leonidov continues to resonate in creative minds. Juror Bonnie Wolf has selected this remarkable computer-generated image by Neubau Architects for her own Award of special distinction. Illustrators Bader and Dilger said simply of their piece: "Little documentation existed about Ivan Leonidov's Lenin Institute project, a student proposal made in 1927. Yet the project has grown in influence within the architectural community. Computer modeling permitted an extended and revived description of this architect's imaginative work"

Ms. Wolf, in praise of this modern-day interpretation, remarked on her attraction "...to the severe and aggressive composition of this work...a drawing which displays great consideration of surface, light, shadow, texture and composition. The fact that it was a computer-generated image came as a surprise and, refreshingly, was of secondary importance."

Given that constructivists extolled the supremacy of the machine, this modern adaptation of Mr. Leonidov's idea proved a fitting subject for a computer illustration. The remote, perhaps clinical, quality of the image's axial composition engaged Ms. Wolf by its "betraying no sense of scale...the sidewalks become highways, structures as we have known them in our own cities become structures which contain cities."

One might sense that Mr. Leonidov, were he alive today, would indeed verify Ms. Wolf's interpretive assessment.

Neubau Imaging
P.O. Box 327
Washington Crossing, Pennsylvania 18977
215.493.4302

David Bader / Curt Dilger

Lenin Institute
Architect: Ivan Leonidov

Computer-rendered image, 10x13, 1993

From the exceptional field of selected entries in *Architecture in Perspective 8*, Juror Walter Netsch singled out a striking watercolor by Houston-based architect, artist and educator, Joyce Rosner, to receive his special Juror's Award. The image is a bold composite of various orthographic views, as well as graphic, artistic interpretations of a design for a small urban park. No stranger to the problems artists face when attempting to graphically portray architectural ideas, Mr. Netsch praised "the drawing's composition, its very delicate attitude toward color, and its juxtaposition of images."

Ms. Rosner elected to employ a graphically referential approach to this illustration problem rather than a simply informational one, thereby enhancing the artistic impact and the layers of meaning it possesses. "The drawing," she stated, "was inspired by old maps which offer a pictorial way of analyzing information. Because the design of *Spark Park* makes such strong references to the forces of nature and the passing of time, a cartographic solution allows the juxtaposition of a variety of elements at varying scales and times of day to create a sense of drama and contradiction within the drawing."

As an accomplished artist in his own right, Juror Netsch cited "elegance of the composition and materials" as the primary basis for his selection of this piece. Furthermore, he was intrigued by the harmony of contradictory images and "elements such as mood and personality that eventually help the drawing transcend from a typical illustration to a very powerful work of art."

4916 Kelvin Street #2
Houston, Texas 77005
713.528.5446

J o y c e   R o s n e r

·I· INCEPTION STONE ·II· EQUINOX LINE ·WALK OF TIME· ·III· CONTEMPLATION BENCH ·IV·WALK OF FAME ·
·V· OBSERVATION CHAIR ·VI· SCULPTURE GNOMON ·VII· SPRING SUMMER FIELD ·VIII· FALL WINTER FIELD ·
·IX· HOURLY BENCH MARKS ·X·WAXING MOON CYCLE FENCE· ·XI· WANING MOON CYCLE FENCE·
·XII· LIGHT PYLONS ·XIII· DAY & NIGHT GATE·

Spark Park
Architects: Robert Morris Architects

Calligraphy by Brody Neuenschwander, Bruges and Belgium.
Watercolor, 32x20, 1992

Moved by the photographic quality of the illustration, Mr. Hedrich selected a powerful watercolor by Dick Sneary as his personal award choice.

For Mr. Hedrich, the visual appeal lay in the way the artist's "elegant and unusual painting treated the foreground, middle ground and picture plane with appropriate attention to detail, variety in light and shadow, and… offsetting of viewpoint to create a very effective composition…" Of comparable importance to Juror Hedrich was "the skillfulness with which the building was placed in context and how that context was illustrated."

Mr. Sneary described his illustration, one of three views for two new entry buildings: "Given the Zoo's location in one of the largest urban parks in the country, a sense of its wooded natural surroundings became an important element in framing an opening into a sunlit clearing where the entry to the zoo was located. Several preliminary ink sketches and watercolor studies were generated from a computer perspective to develop the composition. In layered application of glazes, a sense of depth was created, with the darker, more intense colors in the foreground, and the middle ground was left light, to suggest a bright, sun-drenched building. The tree foliage was also layered with very pale, abstract shapes for the trees behind the buildings, building up to the deep, rich colors in the foreground, with suggestions of individual leaf shapes and bark texture."

It might not be difficult to imagine some envy on the part of Mr. Hedrich who, as a photographer, might have had to wait years for the ideal lighting conditions that Dick Sneary created in this painting. In addition, the illustrator was permitted, in his own words, "to thin the trees sufficiently so that the buildings could be clearly seen, while still giving the impression of looking through a densely wooded grove." Architectural photographers, even of Mr. Hedrich's stature, are rarely allowed this degree of horticultural freedom.

The consummate skill of Mr. Sneary's compositional practice ultimately attracted the experienced compositional eye of photographer Hedrich, who delighted in the painting's "…romantic vision of the architectural form."

323 W. 8th Street, Suite 308
Kansas City, Missouri 64105
816.421.7771

D i c k S n e a r y

Kansas City Zoo Entry
Architects: BNIM Architects

Susan Lynn assisted on this project.
Watercolor, 11x19

The drawings and paintings which comprise the remaining sections present some distinct differences in representational style, emerging from the very process of drawing itself. The first of two categories, as described in the juror's guidelines, was "Formal Presentation Drawings Or Paintings: Complete, finished illustrations of proposed buildings, interiors, or environments of real or imaginary projects, in any medium or size." The intent of distinguishing the submissions was to recognize the vital, energetic, visual appeal of gestural expression and quick idea notation of the "Informal" category, as contrasted by the more structured, studied and elaborate stylistic execution of the "Formal" category. Clearly, the interpretive variables of these guidelines by the submitting artists, the jurors, the competition committee and any reader of this edition may raise questions as to what is appropriate to each category. But unquestionable by any standard is the degree of architectural and aesthetic expression that typifies the following works, regardless of category.

Each artist, with a personal inclination to certain media and technique of drawing derived from their own impulse for expression and, perhaps to an inhibiting, if not constraining degree, from training in the field of architecture or other discipline, attempts to demonstrate the geometrical and spatial qualities of architecture in a verifiable and visually convincing manner. The purpose for doing so is the demonstration of a new design, to either a client or the public, who would more readily understand a pictorial representation of an idea. The result invariably is a "formal" appearance that is well defined and appropriately "attired" for the dress occasion of a presentation. But the richness of imagery typifying these selections shows a delightful interpretive quality that motivates the illustrator's search for a more effective and creative way to tell the architectural story.

20 Prospect Street
Summit, New Jersey 07901
908.277.1909

J a m e s   A k e r s

Proposed Olympic Baseball Venue
Architects: Stang Newdow Architects, Inc.

To capture the excitement and energy of a twilight baseball game, the recurring image was an electric green field glowing under white lights, surrounded in silhouette by the stadium and the lighting trusses. Typical of the artist's process, the painting was reworked an inordinate number of times to assure the intended result—glowing field against dark surround—was met.

Watercolor 16x24, 1992

3700 Lake Shore Drive
Chicago, Illinois 60613
312.404.0798

Manuel Avila

Columbia Exposition Forever

As a commemoration of the 100th anniversary of the 1893 Columbian Exposition, this depiction portrayed themes of fantasy and hope: an assumption that the Colombian Expo was never destroyed and would remain intact well into the future.

Black prismacolor 21x13, 1993

305 Northern Boulevard
Great Neck, New York 11021
516.466.0470

R i c h a r d   C .   B a e h r ,   A I A

Riverside South
Architects: Skidmore, Owings & Merrill, New York

Tempera, 22x50, 1993

Genesis Studios Inc.
225 S. Swoope Avenue, Suite 205
Maitland, Florida 32751
407.539.2606

F r a n k   B a r t u s

Proposed World Trade Center/Orlando, Florida
Architects: VOA Associates Chicago/Orlando

The artist's impressionistic solution dramatically depicted the majestic rise of the tower through cloud layers. The foreground elements enhance the scale of the complex and engage the viewer's imagination of the surroundings. The visual techniques convincingly depicted the form though little design articulation had been accumulated. With an awareness of the encroaching entry of technology into the rendering field, the direction in this presentation provided a union of that technology and artistic craftsmanship.

Gouache on airbrush enhanced photo-print, 1993

27 Chester Drive
Rye, New York 10580.2237
914.698.3129

R o b e r t   B e c k e r

Spectator Light
Architect: Robert Becker

The limitations of load-bearing construction of lighthouses, which out of purpose require height, generated the traditional shapes. Cables using the tensile strength of metals or composites would allow taller structures which would alter these forms. Spectator Light was a study of this more recent technology rising out of the old.
Watercolor, 18x13, 1993

30 St. Felix Street #3A
Brooklyn, New York 11217
718.797.1267

Luis Blanc

Electrifying Skyline

An "electric" sky coloration and an exaggerated convergence were the visually paired prongs conveying the shock of living in a fast-paced dense urban setting.

Prismacolor on illustration board, 11x11, 1992

410.1639 West 2nd Avenue
Vancouver, B.C. Canada V6J 1H3
604.736.7897

L o r i   B r o w n

Great World City, Singapore
Architects: Perkins & Cheung Architects

*The transformation of a retail and entertainment
centre, integral to the architect's design concept,
prompted this Chinese New Year's Festival
imagery, which was carefully overlaid on the
original. The client's antique carousel, which
was part of the design, was also depicted.*
Mixed media, 24x24, 1992

78 Parker Avenue #3
San Francisco, California 94118.2634
415.476.3592

Janet Coral Campbell, AIA

4455 Dunwoody Club Drive

The principal technique was "dropping in" color, in wet-on-slightly-wet 140lb D'arches watercolor paper. As a "faded" version of an original rendering, this second view featured the same perspective of the built-out project. Although rarely required, a fine arts watercolor painting experience was the basis for the series of three artworks.

Watercolor, gesso and pencil, 22x30, 1986

2205 W. Straford Drive
Chandler, Arizona 85224
602.838.0809

D a n i e l   C h i a n g

Eldorado Hotel/Casino Parking Structure Addition
Architects: Mitchell Cohan

To avoid a depiction of a lifeless, massive parking
structure, the building was carefully laid out in
order to blend into the context of the existing hotel.
Both a day-time and this night-time view were
rendered on the same line drawing. The effect of the
night scene was portraying the "heated" atmosphere,
enhanced by various light sources—especially the
"pink neon"—without been over-exaggerated.

Acrylic on the back of clear film, 14x22, 1992

21 Stuyvesant Oval #2E
New York, New York 10009
212.260.4240

Lee Dunnette, AIA

St. Nicholas Sanctuary
Architect: Lee Dunnette, AIA

Designed in 1991 for a site on upper Broadway in NYC, St. Nicholas was an exercise in architectural history and childhood memories, played on a computer. Two years later the design was the basis for this interior rendering. Medieval architecture suggested Durer's woodcuts—rendered in ink. The memory of childhood Christmas suggested the cool/warm palette—rendered in airbrush. For the artist, the result has the mystery and familiarity of an early memory; like the musty smell of grandma's attic.
Ink and airbrush, 20x20, 1993

Buttrick White & Burtis
475 Tenth Avenue
New York, New York 10018
212.967.3333

Michael Middleton Dwyer, AIA

The Charles A. Dana Discovery Center
Architects: Buttrick White & Burtis

Illustrating a proposed new environmental education center on the edge of a lake in New York's Central Park, the drawing was elevated without perspective. The depth was created by the use of shadows and the layering of buildings, trees and walls. The large foreground tree suggested an illusion of perspective. The artist has attempted to create an aura of tranquility around this new structure to be built in one of America's great romantic landscapes.

Color pencil and ink on paper, 22x34, 1990

804 2nd Avenue (Mezzanine)
Seattle, Washington 98104
206.340.0655

B i l l   E v a n s

St. Paul Civic Center
Architects: LMN Seattle/HGA Minneapolis

The station-points of this computer-drawn perspective and photo were precisely aligned to assure an accurate representation. Using opaque watercolor, the Civic Center was painted over a site photograph along with some modifications to the background, improving the overall appearance. The result was then re-photographed for the finished image.

Opaque watercolor, 20x30, 1993

668 Faraone Drive
San Jose, California 95136
408.978.6489

J e f f r e y   M i c h a e l   G e o r g e

New De Anza Hotel
Architect: Jeffrey Michael George

*Created in another era, less restrictive of the
imagination, this architectural fantasy explored
the future possibilities of an existing urban hotel.
The establishment not only accommodates, but
encourages the fantasies of its guests. The design
of the structure was inspired, both formally and
spiritually, by ancient Egyptian civilization.*
Color pencil and pastel, 33x20, 1990

431 S. Dearborn Street, Suite 1001
Chicago, Illinois 60605
312.987.9889

G i l b e r t   G o r s k i

Skyrise
Architects: Skidmore, Owings & Merrill, Chicago

Color pencil and airbrush, 19x12, 1993

7/322 Old Cleveland Road
Coorparoo, Q4151, Australia
061.7.394.4333

J a n e   G r e a l y

Proposed Office Building, Bangkok, Thailand
Architects: Guymer Bailey Architects

A night view was chosen to layer drama, color and movement onto this representation of a corporate headquarters for a leading South East Asian building company. The dynamic, technological orientation of the company was suggested in the main building and subsequently juxtaposed with the traditional, cultural elements of the stone entry.
Gouache, 33x24, 1992

Gordon Grice & Associates
35 Church Street #205
Toronto, Ontario M5E 1T3, Canada
416.536.9191

Gordon Grice, OAA

Deerhurst Highlands Condominium Village
Architects: Zeidler Roberts Partnership

This, the last in a series of nine drawings was commissioned by the developer of a luxury resort community; a companion piece appeared in AIP7. The success of these drawings was largely due to the high degree of collaboration between the illustrator and the architectural design team: Partner-in-charge Ian Grinnell, Designers Rob Eley, Jane Wigle, and Andrea Richardson. While in progress, the drawings were reviewed frequently, allowing the architects to see the buildings emerge in the context of dense forest growth and dramatic topography that characterize the site. Design refinements were then made where appropriate.

Pen and ink on mylar; pencil crayon on mylar reproduction, 21x26, 1992

2839 Paces Ferry Road, Suite 370
Atlanta, Georgia 30339
404.436.0854

D a n   H a r m o n

Jin Mao
Architects: John Portman & Associates

Airbrush on photomural, 72x30, 1993

640 Walavista Avenue
Oakland, California 94610
510.272.9794

Stephan Hoffpauir

At Once the Hair Fell Down...
Architect: Stephan Hoffpauir

Watercolor, color pencil and ink, 16x19, 1993

1501 Western Avenue #500A
Seattle, Washington 98101
206.622.3849

William G. Hook

Swedish Medical Center, Seattle
Architects: NBBJ, Seattle

The architects' design for a main entry wing and new image united a diverse and confusing campus of existing buildings into a coherent medical center. The illustration created a single image which conveyed the design concept, its relationship to the urban setting, and a series of views which visitors would experience in approaching the center and its main lobby.

Transparent watercolor, 35x22, 1992

145 South Olive Street
Orange, California 92666
714.532.3012

Howard Huizing

Idyllwild Retreat
Architect: Howard Huizing

The architectural concept of this cabin retreat combined Craftsman, Oriental and Industrial vernacular, expressing an open but modest floor plan. A consistent palette of color rendered both the structure and its imagined environment, enhancing their integration. A black and white underdrawing enabled the layering of color to freely build up the illustration's earthy atmosphere.
Prismacolor, 9x15, 1993

26 Bacon Street
East Tapinac
Olongapo City 2200, Philippines
222.3286

Angelito Altares Jimenez

Water Tank Gallery
Architect: Shoji Sugioka

*The design scheme concepts of the architect and
the illustrator were originally presented both in
color and charcoal media, but the use of charcoal
media was preferable. The sunrise and foreground
tree provided an effective setting for the building's
simple facade. Direct and reflected sunlight accen-
tuated the cylindrical form and the arches of the
spiral floor structure. The gradual diffusion of
radiating rays to the surrounding environment
suggest an atmosphere of cool, wet Spring.*
Charcoal and pencil, 17x22, 1991

Presentation Techniques
P.O. Box 11173
Knoxville, Tennessee 37939.1173
615.584.8334

David E. Joyner

Hunter Museum of Art
Architects: Derthick, Henley and Wilkerson

Initially executed in pen and ink at a relatively small scale, the perspective was enlarged via a silk screen process onto watercolor paper over which color was applied. This procedure generated two applicable visuals: a line drawing, easily reduced for B&W promotional uses, and a large finished rendering in full color suitable for display.

Watercolor, pen and ink, 20x30, 1992

659 Van Meter Street
Cincinnati, Ohio 45202.1568
513.241.1230

H e l m u t   K i e n t z

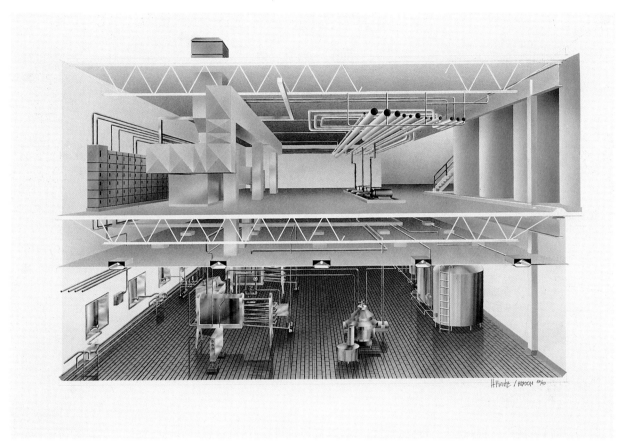

Sanitary Space/Mechanical Space
Architects: Hixson Architecture, Engineering, Interiors

Processing facilities are necessarily highly technical and equipment-oriented. Here, in a one-point interior view, the sanitary filling room and the support utilities above were related together to convey the concept of separate environments. The technical nature of the spaces dictated the use of a line drawing illustrated with opaque watercolor (gouache), and air-brushed to show high levels of detail, especially in the filling room. The mechanical space was intentionally subdued to direct attention to the sanitary space below.

Opaque watercolor and airbrush, 24x36, 1990

741-908 Iwagami-cho Iwagamidori Rokkakusagaru
Nakagyo-Ku
Kyoto, Japan 604
075.802.2291

Hisao Konishi

Police Box of the Cormorant
Architect: Atsushi Ueda

The Police Box of the Cormorant is located by the Bridge of Fire, the nearest of eleven bridges to the Shinkansen tracks on the Murasaki River, Kitakyushu City. In the past, fishing in this river with cormorants and torches would begin at dusk. To reminiscent the old customs, the design motifs of the police box and illumination poles on the bridge suggest a cormorant and torches. Orange Canson paper was used to depict the sky at dusk, the light of illumination and its reflection on the water surface. The clouds, shaped intentionally as an artistic technique, were painted in watercolors. Torches, burning briskly, were airbrushed. As the main feature, the sprayed silver-wall Police Box stands dimly lit at the river bank, guarding the Bridge.
Watercolor and airbrush, 12x18, 1992

217 Pine Street, Suite 1200
Seattle, Washington 98101.1520
206.621.8936

B r u c e   M a c D o n a l d

Paramount Theatre
Client: Ida Cole

With major nearby landmarks brought into view to emphasize the Theatre's fortunate location in the thick of Seattle's downtown office and retail core, a stage set effect was apropos to the subject. The facade below suggested the theatre's rear addition, which will house an extended stage and offices.
Chalk and pencil, 1993

13 Quai Du Commerce
69009 Lyon, France
33.78.64.83.59

Philippe Martyniak

Deree College, Greece
Architects: A. Anthony Tappe and Associates

Initially planned as an aerial view of this college library addition, and against the architect's apprehension that his client might be confused by multiple imagery because of the drawing's fundraising purpose, a "competition style" rendering was chosen nonetheless. The result developed quickly, and a new commission for a inner space illustration with the same approach was similarly prepared.

Pastel and color pencil, 30x20, 1992

Santa Maria 317 Constitution Street
Mosta MST 03, Malta
356.412829

Iain McFarlane

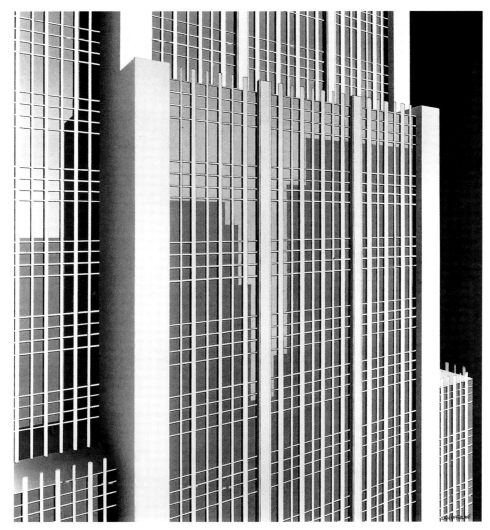

Miglin-Beitler Tower, Chicago
Architects: Cesar Pelli & Associates

With what was anticipated to be the tallest building in the world, there was a strong temptation to show the building in its entirety. But as an alternative presentation, a carefully chosen point was selected for this particular image (one of several), indicating only part of the facade at a given height, but in greater detail than would have been possible with an overall view. The intent was not to create an artistic night-time scene, but a photorealistic representation of the building as itself by using varying shades to create relatively strong shadows and reflections. The theme was continued by using a black background rather than a contextual cityscape.

Airbrush, liquid watercolor on line board, 19x18, 1993

1639 W. 2nd Avenue #410
Vancouver B. C. Canada V6J 1H3
604.683.1622

R o b e r t M c I l h a r g e y

Hotel & Convention Centre & Malaysiana, Johor Bahru
Architects: Arthur Erickson Architectural Corporation, Hijjas Kasturi Associates,
Aitken Wreglesworth Associates and Atelier M.

Mixed media, 22x24, 1992

223 Indian Road Crescent
Toronto, Canada M6P 2G6
416.763.1387

Michael B. Morrissey

Kowloon Point Development Competition
Architects: Webb Zerafa Menkes Housden Architects, Toronto

Airbrush, 18x24, 1992

3757 Main Highway, P.O. Box 378
Miami, Florida 33133
305.446.8159

Orest Associates

Embarcadero Waterfront Competition
Architects: Architecture Orest

Tempera, 24x20, 1992

P.O. Box 51343
Pacific Grove, California 93950
408.384.7781

A l e x a n d e r   O r t e n b e r g

Background for the 'Season's Greetings' Card

*To convey the festive spirit of the Holiday
Season as seen through an architect's eye, the
illustration presents several contrasts—wine
and cake set on top of the "drawing", next to
drafting tools; the clash of the "drawing's"
cold winter colors and the warm, soft
"objects," which accentuate the atmosphere
of creative and eventful chaos, so typical for
an architectural office.*

Prismacolor, ink wash and watercolor, 16x12, 1992

909 E. Water Street
Urbana, Illinois 61801
217.333.1992

J e f f r e y   S .   P o s s

Prospect and Refuge
Architect: Jeffrey S. Poss

The midwestern house depicted in this drawing was conceived as both a geometric construct, and a mounded extension of its prairie site. The portrayal emphasized two archetypal attributes of dwelling: the desire for an unimpeded opportunity to (prospect), and the desire for a place of concealment (refuge).
Pastel and pencil, 27x36, 1992

410.1639 West 2nd Avenue
Vancouver B.C. Canada V6J 1H3
604.736.5430

Eugene V. Radvenis

West Coast Meeting House
Architects: Acton Johnson Ostry Architects

The design of the West Coast Meeting House reflects the evolution of Coast Salish architecture and alludes to the significant story of the Saanich Peoples' Great Flood. Against the background of Sacred Mountain, the buildings wind around natural rock outcroppings and an outdoor gathering space—the Sacred Circle, a sunken fire pit providing a place for the telling of stories. The seating winds around the fire pit in a spiral manner, reflecting the legend of the coiled cedar rope which secured canoes of the Saanich ancestors to Sacred Mountain during the Great Flood. The rendering's purpose was to convey a sense of the history and traditions of the Native Peoples as well as their vision for the future.

Airbrush, marker and pencil crayon, 30x18, 1992

8600 Indian Hills Drive
Omaha, Nebraska 68114
402.391.8111

Philip Sampson

Lincoln University Library
Architects: Leo A. Daly Company

*One of two renderings, an evening
aerial view was an effective second
choice for featuring the open, reflective,
and illuminated contemporary characteristics of a new library. This is a
collaboration with Scott Nordstrom.*
Ink and gouache, 18x28, 1991

7740 Dean Road
Indianapolis, Indiana 46240
317.595.0016

E r i c   S c h l e e f

Ochsner Residence, Timber Cove, California
Architect: Joan Hallberg, AIA

To generate an illustration of the proposed structure, site and adjacent neighbors, the layout was derived from a computer perspective, the architect's drawing, site maps and photos. Color was applied to a pencil rendering photocopied on Strathmore medium surface paper. Pastel, in powder form, was rubbed on with cotton in layers and sprayed lightly each time with fixative to achieve the desired intensity. Colored pencil and watercolor added texture and detail. Terry Steadham collaborated on this project.

Pastel, pencil and watercolor on paper, 8x15, 1993

31.8.213 Honcho
Wakoshi, Saitamaken
Japan 351.01
048.465.6554.1615

Hideo Shirai

Miyagi Arena
Architects: Taisei Corporation

Airbrush, pen and ink, 16x24, 1993

1806 8th Avenue #212
Seattle, Washington 98101
206.223.5244

Slava M. Simontov

Villa Simonyi
Architect: Wendell Lovett, FAIA

The angles and fluid movement of the Villa Simonyi, a modern "tower house" by a lake, are linked with the movement of a nautical seascape. The suggestion of a cool evening feeling, contrasted with the quasi-religious sky reflections, achieved a three-dimensional effect, using airbrush and watercolor techniques. With a typical northwest sunset inferred on the glass front facade, the result was an exciting, articulate "ship of the land," honestly and joyfully portrayed.
Watercolor and airbrush, 30x42, 1993

115 Fifth Avenue
New York, New York 10003
212.353.4684

Thomas F. Singer

Lobby View
Architects: Haines Lundberg Waehler

Modernist spaces pose a special challenge to the illustrator due to their broad flat surfaces and unadorned furnishings, which combine to form a neutral background for the play of light and reflections. These effects were simulated with the use of the computer. The architecture and furnishings had their forms and surfaces defined with respect to five discrete light sources. Raytracing software was used to study their interaction, the adjustments resulting in this projection. The image was produced using Microstation and Modelview software and an Interpro 340 Workstation by Intergraph Corporation.
CADD, 12x24, 1992

8 South Michigan Avenue, #310
Chicago, Illinois 60603
312.580.1995

R a e l   S l u t s k y

Larabee Commons Townhomes-Courtyard
Architects: Pappageorge/Haymes

An unusual viewpoint from within a new townhome apartment person-
alized the image of a large building complex, and imparted a sense of
domesticity to the scene. Diaphanous curtains both framed and softened a view that belies the earthbound gravity of rough masonry walls
surrounding an open courtyard below. Several vignettes of families on
private balconies or terraces and children of different ages playing in the
courtyard reinforced the home-like atmosphere. The bright, sunny
atmosphere allowed the artist to feature the modeled character of split-
face block surfaces as well as sharply defined shadows pinpointing the
architectural accents of copper scuppers and downspouts.

Felt-tip pen and color pencil on vellum, 18x24, 1987

The Studio of James C. Smith
700 South Clinton Street
Chicago, Illinois 60607
312.987.0132

James C. Smith

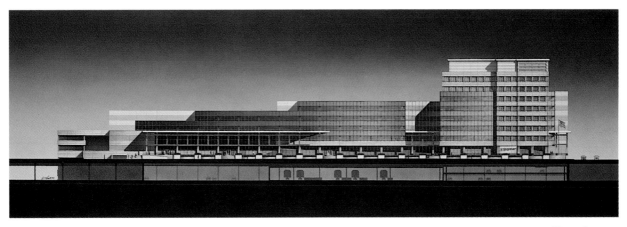

New Main Post Office, Chicago
Architects: Knight Architects Engineers Planners

Influenced by Arata Isozaki's images, particularly 'The Brooklyn Museum' and 'The Disney Building,' this painting portrayed the Post Office elevation in a dramatic sense of light, color and material. The green glass was complimented by the subtle violet chroma of the background. The sheer magnitude of the project was emphatically conveyed by the oversize dimensions of the painting.
Airbrush, 28x84, 1991

361 W. Chestnut, Suite 2N
Chicago, Illinois, 60610
312.951.1656

Tainer Associates Ltd.

Park Lincoln—Interior
Architects: Pappageorge/Haymes Ltd.

Utilizing the viewpoint of a prospective buyer's tour, colors, shading, and the placement of objects helped infuse a human touch in this apartment perspective, and make a typically small area seem much larger. The musical instruments added the necessary decorative elements. A variety of techniques including marker, air brush, pencil, paint and sponge, was used to give richness to a very simple interior.
Mixed media, 24x24, 1988

672 Grove Street
Newton, Massachusetts 02162
617.332.7885

Mongkol Tansantisuk

TBI River Villa
Architects: Cambridge Seven Associates

The lighting for this project in Bangkok, Thailand was of major concern for both the client and the architect. The night scene was selected to emphasize the verticality of the building through illuminated fenestration and lively activities along the waterfront. The scale of the building was reinforced by the pavilion and entourage at ground level.

Color pencil on black board, 20x20, 1993

407.1509 Centre Street S.W.
Calgary, Alberta
403.262.4383

R e n e   T h i b a u l t

The Crystalline
Conceptual Design: Rene Thibault

*The inspiration behind "The Crystalline" was visualizing
architecture as influenced by elements in nature rather than
by historic or current architectural disciplines. In essence,
Nature might induce a timelessness to such a concept. The
monumental simplicity of the complex was dramatized with
the light of a winter's evening, reflected in the multiple
surfaces of the structure. Rolling mounds and delicate trees
softened the angularity of the emerging crystals.*

Mixed media, 22x14, 1992

2.1005.2.6, Mihara-dai
Sakai-shi, Japan 590.01
0722.97.2528

Koji Watanabe

N-Project
Architects: Takenaka Corporation

For this large-scale retail perspective, drawn under a limited time of three days, the client's assignment was to generate an image of an inspiring facility, while giving the artist limitless options for the best expression. Rather than projecting minute details at this stage, a picturesque approach in an oil painting motif had been proposed and a painting knife technique with acrylic color was applied to describe the various elements while still suggesting high resolution.
Acrylic color, 27x19,

922 Milwood Avenue
Venice, California 90291
310.821.8189

Curtis James Woodhouse

Playa Vista Office Campus
Architects: Moore Ruble Yudell Architects & Planners

Within a series of seven images produced for both marketing and design studies, this view features several related yet varied courtyard spaces, set against a backdrop of fairly standard buildings. A simple pencil on vellum line drawing was copied onto Canson paper and dry-mounted to foam-core for painting. The evening scene added interest to the series and represented an "after hours" component of the project.

Watercolor and photocopy on Canson paper, 7x12, 1992

Tamotsu Yamamoto

The Large Glass (Hancocked Tower)
Architect: Marcel Duchamp

Marcel Duchamp added a moustache and goatee to a reproduction of the most famous painting in the world, Leonardo DaVinci's masterpiece, the "Mona Lisa" and called it "Assisted readymade". Years later, he signed an unaltered print of the Mona Lisa, subtitling it "Rasee"—French for "shaved".

Pencil, 30x40, 1990

120 N.W.Parkway
Kansas City, Missouri 64150
816.587.9500

A a r o n K . Z i m m e r m a n

Katewood Shores Retirement Center
Architects: WRS, Kansas City

In response to the design intent, the play of light and shadow of the natural wooded site, as well as the warmth and texture of indigenous materials, became the points of emphasis for the painting. The view was selected to highlight a primary juncture of program spaces—the commons building with porte cochere, living units, and one of a series of "pavilions" which punctuate secondary entrance locations and offer vistas over the lake. The layout was composed with Autocad Release 12 and rendered in ink and watercolor.

Watercolor, 14x25, 1993

The published reference describing work that would qualify for selection in this category read: "Informal Sketches Or Conceptual Design Drawings: Sketches, design concept, and process drawings of proposed building, interiors, or environments of real or imaginary projects, in any medium or size." What has remained problematic since categories were first introduced to ASAP's competition is the difficulty of distinguishing form from content, although both may likely be intertwined.

The unbridled energy of intuitive response that suffuses an engaging sketch image has generally been acknowledged as a purer expression of concept or idea. In bridling the unrestrained power of inspiration, which is sometimes so forceful that the archetypal model of a two-inch doodle on the back of an envelope or a paper napkin best records what could be considered a form of architectural DNA, the enlivening seed of design creation, it really makes no difference what the capturing medium is. If such an impulsive, non-thinking response is the mode for solving the problem at hand (literally and figuratively), it also makes no difference whether it is a "design" problem or a "perspective" problem. The integrity of a search for a solution is similarly untainted in both cases. The jurors were keen enough to sense something of these forces in the works chosen for the informal category. Their decisions, as the pieces themselves, may encourage the reader to determine if indeed such forceful energy lay within the gestural strength of the following images.

Richard Bergmann Architects
63 Park Street
New Canaan, Connecticut 06840
203.966.9505

R i c h a r d   B e r g m a n n ,   F A I A

Working Garden for Children, New York Botanical Garden
Architects: Richard Bergmann Architects

One of a series of pen-and-ink semi-abstract drawings illustrated the proposed project as a strong graphic image, simple to remember, and that would reproduce easily in black and white. The drawing also had to convey a convincing sense of reality, and without seeming to be a final design, purposely indicated the brick detailing.
Pen and ink, 12x12, 1985

13b Pauline Street
Winthrop, Massachusetts 02152
617.846.4766

Frank M. Costantino

Olympics 2000, Istanbul
Architects: Stang Newdow Architects, Inc.

Generated over a light blue freehand perspective framework to establish proportions, the red pencil sketch helped suggest details of a proposed gymnasium's major components. The study, emphasizing one corner of a symmetrically designed facility, was prepared as one of four sketch analyses and better demonstrates its enormous scale, without diminishing key features of the principal forms. With but minor adjustments, the final projected drawing was markedly similar to this initial impression.

Color pencil, 7x10, 1992

136 1/2 South Main Street Studio One
Bowling Green, Ohio 43402
419.352.4740

D u d l e y   M .   F l e m i n g

Zimmer Executive Building
Architects: Schenkel Shultz

As one of three views capturing the essence of the building's design, without relying on detail or structure, this piece was conceptualized in one day from the architect's verbal input. Primarily, the drawing portrayed a believable high volume space, while suggesting the relationship between interior and exterior, with its use of glass and other materials. A dramatic composition was achieved by emphasizing the building's sharp perspective angle.

Pencil, watercolor and chalk, 30x24, 1989

601 4th Street #112
San Francisco, California 94107
415.243.4394

Christopher Grubbs

Project, Japan
Architects: Projects International, Hawaii

Prismacolor on copy of original drawing, 6x10, 1993

Architectural Renderings
1162 Charm Acres Place
Pacific Palisades, California 90272
310.573.1155

D o u g l a s   E .   J a m i e s o n

Iwaki Resort Masterplan
Architects: A.C. Martin and Associates

Watercolor and pencil, 11x8, 1991

Ringman Design & Illustration
2700 Fairmount Street Suite 100
Dallas, Texas 75201
214.871.9001

Samuel Ringman

Arena
Architect: Samuel Rngman

Analogous of the architect's struggle against forces beyond his control, it was important to render the image as a fantasy piece—a monochromatic approach with watercolor emphasized its surrealism.

Watercolor and pencil, 7x7, 1991

Ulmenstrasse 40
2000 Hamburg 60, Germany
40.48061848

Sergei E. Tchoban

The Life on the Backside of the Town
Architect: Sergei E. Tchoban

Only a courtyard, found in every big town…the pen and sepia-ink technique, the combination of scales and different views, continued into each other, of the facades, of the architectural style, helps project an image of the mysterious life in this little house on the backside of the town…

Watercolor, pen and ink, 24x24, 1993

202 Parkland Avenue
St. Louis, Missouri 63122
314.821.9285

R o b e r t G . W a t e l , J r .

Entrance to the Muny Opera
Architects: Hellmuth, Obata & Kassabaum

One of eight illustrations to communicate the proposed renovation of a landmark outdoor performing arts facility, the approach for the sketches was a viewer's tour explaining each area's distinct architectural characteristics. The atmospheres in the views progressed from twilight into starlit darkness, eliciting the verdant, balmy ambience familiar to patrons of this traditional St. Louis summer evening's entertainment.

Watercolor, pen and ink, 8x12, 1992

P a r t i c i p a n t s

The following members submitted entries for consideration

Alternates

Ernest Burden	Brooklyn, New York	718-768-7495
Barbara Worth Ratner	Atlanta, Georgia	404-876-3943
Mike Burroughs	Bainbridge Is. Washington	206-780-9406
Rod L. Booze	Dallas, Texas	214-520-3311
Richard Chenoweth	Silver Spring, Maryland	301-589-0336
Robert Comazzi	Watertown, Massachusetts	617-926-3300
Elizabeth Ann Day	Austin, Texas	512-472-2580
Yoshie L. Ideno	Tokyo, Japan	03-3263-4813
Dominick Durante, AIA	Cleveland, Ohio	216-881-2444
Jennifer England	Miami, Florida	305-446-8159
Les Leffingwell	New Berlin, Wisconsin	414-782-4808
Eric Hyne	Odenton, Maryland	410-551-5405
Mark E. Lawrence	Laguna Niguel, California	
Sun-Ho Lee	Seoul, Korea	02-334-2118˙
Paul Lukez	Boston, Massachusetts	617-227-2735
Barbara Morello	Vienna, Austria	222-320-9744
Steve Oles, FAIA	Newton, Massachusetts	617-527-6790
Henry E. Sorenson, Jr.	Bozeman, Montana	406-587-7113
Voytek Szczepanski	Fort Lauderdale, Florida	305-485-2528

Officers

Dario Tainer, AIA	President	312 951-1656
Rael Slutsky, AIA	Vice President	312 580-1995
Tamotsu Yamamoto	Treasurer	617 542-1021
Frank M. Costantino	Secretary	617 846-4766
Dan Harmon	Member-at-Large	404 436-0854
Gordon Grice, OAA, MRAIC	President Emeritus	416 536-9191
Robert A. Costantino	Counsel	617 569-8870

Advisory Council

Dan Harmon, Chairman	Atlanta, Georgia	404 436-0854
Bill Ross	Calgary, Canada	403 255-6486
Susan Austin-Salvo	Exton, Pennsylvania	215 692-9591
Richard Ferrier, AIA	Arlington, Texas	817 273 2801
Jeffrey M. George	San Jose, California	408 978-6489
William Hook	Seattle, Washington	206 622-3849
Robert LeMond, FAIA	Fort Worth, Texas	817 926-3433
Michael McCann	Toronto Ontario	416 964-7532
Paul Stevenson Oles, FAIA	Boston, Massachusetts	617 527-6790
Richard Rochon	Dearborn, Michigan	313 584-9580
Thomas W. Schaller, AIA	New York, New York	212 362-5524
Robert Watel, Jr.	St. Louis, Missouri	314 965-9203

International Coordinators

Ricardo Almazan	Mexico	52-5-523-6015
Octavio Balda	Germany	040-395-112
Robert W. Gill	Australia	61-3-240-1322
Miguelangel Gutierrez	Mexico	52-5-553-2169
Young Ki	Korea	312-580-1995
Dario Tainer, AIA	Italy	312 951-1656
Shane O'Toole	Ireland	353-1-602-750
Robert Voticky, RIBA, SAI	England	44-81-940-3819
Nobuo Kadowaki, JARA	Japan	81-3-3401-5877
Shu-Xiang Xi	China	

Inquiries on membership in the Society, additional copies of **AIP 8** or previous years' catalogues, orders for the hardcover title, *Architecture In Perspective, A Five-Year Retrospective of Award-Winning Illustration*, or general information may be obtained by writing or phoning ASAP at the address below. Prospective members may also contact an Officer, Advisory Councillor or an International Coordinator nearest their location to learn more about the Society, its activities, benefits and exhibition schedule.

ASAP, 320 Newbury Street Boston, MA 02115 • 617-846-4766

The American Society of Architectural Perspectivists (ASAP) was founded in 1986 as an organization to foster communication among the nation's architectural perspectivists, to raise the standards of design drawing and to acquaint a broader public with the importance of such drawing as an adjunct to architectural design. Membership in the Society is not limited to professional illustrators only, but is open to architects, designers, students—anyone engaged in the serious pursuit of drawing as a design or presentation tool in architecture.

The single principle means of achieving the goals of the Society is an annual competitive exhibition and convention, which brings together the current works and practitioners of architectural drawing from around the world. The works are selected from submissions by a jury of respected professionals from the fields of architecture, illustration and design education. Although a number of pieces are selected for exhibition and inclusion in the annual ASAP catalogue, the drawing judged to be that year's most outstanding work may be accorded the highest award of the Society—and indeed the most prestigious in the field of architectural drawing—The Hugh Ferriss Memorial Prize.

In addition to sponsoring the travelling exhibitions, ASAP, in coordination with the American Institute of Architects, serves as a national clearing house and referral agency for architects and developers seeking the services of perspectivists. The Society's continental and international communication network provides the means for any of its members to sustain professional liason with their counterparts in Britain's Society Of Architectural Illustrators, the Japan Architectural Renderers Association, and nine different countries around the world.

The central purpose of ASAP remains the improvement of architectural drawing in North America and worldwide. By recognizing, celebrating, and disseminating the highest achievements in the illustration of buildings, the Society continues to demonstrate that the quality of the work—and the working—will be further heightened. With more sensitive, more accurate, and more aesthetic characteristics, the field of architectural illustration—and its end, architecture—will be continually enhanced, providing benefit for all of us.

The American Society of Architectural Perspectivists
320 Newbury Street Boston, MA 02115 • 617-846-4766